MW01490985

The Slow Cooker Soup Cookbook

EASY SLOW-COOKER SOUP RECIPES

BY

MARTHA STONE

Disclaimer

The information and recipes contained within The Slow Cooker Soup Cookbook are based on extensive research conducted by the author. The sources used for the research are credible and authentic to the best of our knowledge. In no event shall the author be liable for any direct, indirect, incidental, punitive, or consequential damages of any kind whatsoever with respect to the service, the materials and the products contained within. This eBook is not a substitute for professional nutritional or culinary advice.

For a complete list of my published books, please, visit my Author's Page...

http://www.amazon.com/Martha-Stone/e/B00FDU8GR6/

You can also check out my blog at:
http://martha-stone.blogspot.com

or my Facebook at:
https://www.facebook.com/marthastone2013

Table of Contents

Slow Cooker Soups: A Savory and Delicious Meal that Will Make Your Mouth Water

If you like cooking but don't find it convenient with your busy schedule and work, what you really need is a slow cooker. Nothing can add more convenience to cooking as this smart cooking device. All you have to do is add the ingredients and leave them to cook when you leave for work, and you will have your meal ready by the time you are back.

However, convenience is not all that a slow cooker can bring to your cooking; it also brings out the natural flavors of foods to be savored and saves you a lot of money that you spend on eating out. While all your meals are going to turn out extremely delicious in a slow cooker, soups are often the best when cooked this way.

When you cook soup and stock in slow cookers, it allows the natural flavor of the meat and vegetables to come out at its best, giving your soup an unmatchable taste. And with these cookers, it's hardly ever possible to go wrong with your soup; there is little chance you can burn it or overcook it.

To help you make the best soups, here are 25 simple slow cooker soup recipes that you can easily try at home. We are sure they will turn out to be extremely delicious and you will simply love having these wonderful soups on your dinner table time and again. So, do try out these soups, and enjoy the hearty and flavorful food that slow cookers can make.

The Recipes

We won't waste any more of your time and start off with the recipes right away.

1. Beef Vegetable Barley Soup

A classic mix of meat, vegetables and grains, this wonderful soup is only served delicious!

Ingredients:

- 2 meaty beef shanks
- ½ lbs. stew meat cut in cubes
- 2 ribs of sliced celery with tops
- 1 ½ cup frozen peas
- 1 diced large onion
- 2 cups thinly sliced carrots
- 1 cup frozen green beans
- 2 minced garlic cloves
- 1 can of diced tomatoes (14.5 oz)
- ¾ cup lima beans
- 1 bay leaf
- 1 ½ tsp. salt
- 1 tbsp. dried parsley
- 2 tsp. dried basil
- 2 medium peeled and diced potatoes
- ¼ cup barley
- 4 to 5 cup beef broth

Preparation Time: 10-12 hours
Yields: Serves 4 or more

Instructions:

1. For this recipe, you will need a 6 quart slow cooker.
2. In the slow cooker, put everything except the barley and add water, filling the slow cooker to 1 ½ inches. Leave it to cook for 8 to 10 hours on low.
3. Two hours before serving, take out the soup bone from the pot, chop away the meat from it and add the meat back to the cooker.
4. Add barley and cook the soup on high until the barley gets tender. Serve hot.

2. Bean Soup with Ham

Ready in a snap and wonderful to taste, this Northern style soup is definitely one of the best to try with slow cookers.

Ingredients:

- 8 oz. Great Northern beans (soak them overnight and drain in the morning)
- 2 can of tomato sauce (8 oz. each)
- 4 cups water
- 2 diced potatoes
- 2 small chopped onions
- 2 shredded carrots
- Salt and pepper to taste
- 1 cup diced ham

Preparation Time: 9 – 11 hours
Yields: Serves 4

Instructions:

1. In a pot, add fresh water and beans and bring them to a boil. Lower the heat and let the beans simmer for 30 minutes.
2. Drain the beans and put them in the slow cooker with all other ingredients. Cook for 8 to 10 hours on low. Check the seasoning and serve hot.

3. Broccoli and Cheese Soup

Another wonderful slow cooker soup, this can be made even more wonderful if served with tossed salad.

Ingredients:

- 1 packet frozen broccoli (10 oz.), chopped and thawed
- 2 cups cooked noodles
- 2 cups American cheese, finely shredded
- ¼ cup chopped onion
- 5 cups milk
- Salt to taste
- 1 tbsp. flour
- 2 tbsp. butter

Preparation Time: 3 to 4 hours
Yields: Serves 8

Instructions:

1. Add all the ingredients in a slow cooker and stir them well together.
2. Cook for 3 to 4 hours on low. You can add more milk if the soup is too thick. Serve hot.

4. Country Style Chicken Soup

With the natural flavors of vegetables, chicken and wonderful seasonings, this soup is going to be a treat for your taste buds.

Ingredients:

- 1 whole fryer chicken weighing 2 ½ to 3 lbs.
- 4 cups chicken stock
- 1 cup uncooked noodles
- 3 sliced carrots
- 2 chopped onions
- 2 sliced celery stalks
- 1 ½ cup frozen peas
- A dash of dried thyme leaves
- 2 tsp. salt
- ½ tsp. dried basil
- ¼ tsp. pepper
- 3 tbsp. dried parsley flakes

Preparation Time: 9 to 11 hours
Yields: Serves 4

Instructions:

1. Add all the ingredients except the noodles into the slow cooker and cook for 8 to 10 hours on low.
2. An hour before serving, take out the chicken from the pot, remove the meat and add the meat back to the cooker.
3. Add the noodles and cook on high for another hour. Serve hot.

5. Onion Soup

With cheese and delicious seasonings, this wonderful onion soup is going to be delectable.

Ingredients:

- 3 cups sliced onions
- 1 cup Mozzarella or Parmesan cheese
- 4 cups beef broth
- ¼ cup dry Cognac or Vermouth
- 1 baguette French bread
- ¼ cup butter
- 1 tsp. salt
- 2 tbsp. flour
- 1 tbsp. sugar

Preparation Time: 15 hours
Yields: Serves 6

Instructions:

1. Slice the French bread in 1-inch thick pieces.
2. Put the broth in the slow cooker and let it cook on high.
3. In the meantime, add butter to a large skillet and cook the onions in it for about 20 minutes.
4. Add salt and sugar and cook until the onions are browned. Add the flour next and cook for a minute.
5. Add onions and Vermouth/Cognac to the slow cooker with the broth. Let if cook on high for 3 hours.

6. When serving, ladle the soup into bowls, and sprinkle with cheese and a piece of French bread.

6. Taco Soup

Make it with turkey or lean beef, both ways this recipe is simple and extremely mouth-watering!

Ingredients:

- 1 ½ lbs. turkey or ground round
- 1 can of un-drained corn
- 1 can of un-drained kidney beans
- 1 can of un-drained black beans
- 1 can of tomato sauce
- 2 cans of chopped tomatoes
- 1 large chopped onion
- 2 tbsp. oil
- 1 envelope taco seasoning

Preparation Time: 7 hours
Yields: Serves 6 to 8

Instructions:

1. Heat oil in a pan and add onions to it, cooking until the onions are tender. Add the meat and continue to cook until it is no longer pink in color. Drain well.
2. Put the meat in the slow cooker with all the other ingredients and stir well. Cook for 4 to 6 hours on low. Serve with shredded cheese and taco chips.

7. Crab Soup

If seafood is what you love most, this crab soup made in a slow cooker is definitely going to be one of your favorites.

Ingredients:

- 2 cups flaked and picked crabmeat
- ½ cup saltine crackers
- 2 cups half-and-half
- 2 cups milk
- 2 strips of lemon peel
- 3 tbsp. butter
- 2 tbsp. dry sherry
- ¼ tsp. ground nutmeg
- Salt and pepper to taste

Preparation Time: 5 hours
Yields: Serves 6 to 8

Instructions:

1. Add all the ingredients except crackers and sherry to the slow cooker and mix them well. Cook for 4 to 5 hours on low.
2. Stir in the cracker crumbs and sherry just before serving. You can also add cooked shrimps 30 minutes before you serve the soup to add variation.

8. Potato Soup

If you like everything to do with potatoes, try this slow cooker potato soup and you'll love them even more.

Ingredients:

- 3 lbs. peeled and cubed potatoes
- 1 can cream of celery soup
- 1 can cheddar cheese soup
- 1 can of water (equivalent to a soup can)
- 8 slices of sliced and cooked bacon
- 1 cup chopped green onions
- ¼ cup chopped parsley
- ¼ cup chopped red bell pepper
- 2 tsp. chicken bouillon granules
- Dash of thyme
- Ground black pepper to taste

Preparation Time: 9 hours
Yields: Serves 4

Instructions:

1. Add all the ingredients except thyme and parsley to the slow cooker. Cook for 7 to 9 hours on low.
2. In the last hour of cooking, add thyme and parsley and continue to cook on low. Serve hot.

9. Winter Squash Soup

Extremely quick and easy to make, this soup can be turned into a vegetarian recipe by using vegetable broth.

Ingredients:

- 2 packets frozen winter squash puree (10 oz. each)
- 1 cup chopped onions
- 1 cup chicken broth
- ¾ cup heavy cream
- ½ tsp. salt
- ½ tsp. dried leaf thyme
- ¼ tsp. dried leaf sage
- Ground black pepper to taste

Preparation Time: 5 hours
Yields: Serves 4

Instructions:

1. Add chicken broth, squash puree, onions and seasonings to the slow cooker and let cook for 4 to 5 hours on low. Add cream and cook for another 15 minutes.
2. In small batches, blend the soup until it gets a smooth texture. Adjust the seasonings and serve hot.

10. Lentil Soup

Serve this simple and delicious soup with freshly baked biscuits or cornbread, and this will be one of the heartiest meals you have had in your life.

Ingredients:

- ½ cup chopped onions
- 2 cups dried lentils
- ½ cup chopped celery
- 8 cups water
- ¼ cups chopped carrots
- 1 can of tomatoes (14.5 oz.)
- 1 clove crushed garlic
- 1 ½ tbsp. crumbled bacon
- 3 tbsp. snipped parsley
- 2 tbsp. wine vinegar
- 2 ½ tsp. salt
- ½ tsp. dried leaf oregano
- ¼ tsp. ground black pepper

Preparation Time: 10 hours
Yields: Serves 4

Instructions:

1. Rinse the lentils and add them to the slow cooker. Add all other ingredients except the vinegar and tomatoes to the slow cooker as well. Cook on low for 8 to 10 hours.
2. Add vinegar and tomatoes and cook on high for an additional 15 minutes. Serve hot.

11. Tomato Vegetable Soup

Served with crusty bread or muffins, this soup is another hearty delight that you can try for dinnertime.

Ingredients:

- 1 quart broth (mushroom, vegetable or chicken)
- 1 can stewed tomatoes (14.5 oz.)
- 1 can tomatoes (14.5 oz.)
- 1 can un-drained black beans (16 oz.)
- ¼ cup long grain rice
- ½ head chopped cabbage
- 2 sliced celery ribs
- 1 finely chopped jalapeno pepper
- 1 medium chopped onion
- 2 finely chopped carrots
- Salt and black pepper to taste

Preparation Time: 5 hours
Yields: Serves 4 to 6

Instructions:

1. In a Dutch oven pan, mix together the broth, carrots, onion, celery and tomato, and bring it to a boil. Let it simmer for 15 minutes.
2. Put this vegetable mixture into the slow cooker along with rice, black beans and jalapeno. Cook for 5 hours on low.

12. White Bean Soup

When cooked in a slow cooker, this hearty bean soup can turn out to be very tasty, especially when served with freshly baked cornbread.

Ingredients:

- 2 smoked ham hocks
- 1 ½ cup sliced celery
- 1 ½ cup sliced carrots
- 1 quart vegetable broth
- 1 medium diced onion
- 2 cans diced tomatoes with juice (14.5 oz.)
- ½ cup corn kennels
- 1 cup cooked and drained frozen baby lima beans
- 3 cans drained white beans (15 oz. each)
- ½ tsp. dried thyme
- ¼ tsp. ground black pepper
- Salt to taste

Preparation Time: 9 hours
Yields: Serves 8 to 10

Instructions:

1. In a slow cooker, add ham hocks, carrots, onions, celery and broth. Cook on low for 8 hours.
2. Strain the broth and remove excess fat. Put the broth back into the slow cooker. Take out the ham hocks, remove the meat from bones, dice it and return it to the cooker. Add the remaining ingredients and seasonings, and cook for an hour on high. Serve hot.

13. Lamb Meat Ball Soup

Lamb has a truly unique and remarkable taste, and this slow cooker soup recipe brings it out.

Ingredients:

- ½ cup chopped onions
- ¼ cup lentils
- 1 chopped celery rib
- 1 chopped carrot
- 6 cups beef stock
- ¼ cup chicken stock
- 1 can diced tomatoes (14.5 oz.)
- 1 lb. ground lamb meat
- 1 tbsp. chopped parsley
- 1 minced garlic clove
- 1 tsp. salt
- 4 tbsp. all-purpose flour
- ¼ tsp. pepper
- ½ tsp. cumin
- 1 tsp. freshly grated ginger
- 2 tbsp. vegetable oil

Preparation Time: 6 hours
Yields: Serves 6

Instructions:

1. In a saucepan, put lentils and cover them with water. Bring to a boil and keep it boiling for about 3 minutes. Remove from the heat and let it cool for about an hour. Put it back on heat and simmer for

45 minutes. Drain the lentils and add them to the slow cooker.

2. In a large skillet, heat the oil and add onions to saute over medium heat. Add carrots and celery and cook until the onion turns tender. Add these vegetables to the slow cooker as well. Add ginger, tomatoes, salt, pepper, cumin and beef stock to the cooker, and cook on low for 3 ½ hours.

3. In a bowl, mix ground lamb, salt, flour, garlic, parsley and chicken stock together. Make small balls from this mix and add them to the slow cooker. Cook for an additional 1 ½ hours. Serve hot.

14. Mexican Beef and Bean Soup

If you are in the mood to try something simple but spicy. This easy-to-make Mexican soup is the perfect pick for you.

Ingredients:

- 1 lb. ground beef
- 1 can refried beans
- 1 cup chopped onions
- 1 can cheddar cheese soup
- 1 can chili beef soup
- 2 cans diced tomatoes (14.5 oz. each)
- 2 can Rotel tomatoes

Preparation Time: 5 hours
Yields: Serves 4

Instructions:

1. In a pan, brown onions and ground beef. Add this to the slow cooker along with all the other ingredients. Cook for 3 to 5 hours on low. You can add a bit of water if it gets too thick. Serve hot.

15. Chicken and Pasta Soup

If you are looking for a completely unique and slightly Italian taste, this soup is definitely worth a try.

Ingredients:

- 2 cups cooked and diced chicken
- 3 cans chicken broth (10.5 oz. each)
- 1 can diced tomatoes with juice (14.5 oz.)
- 1 cup water
- 1 cup chopped onions
- 1/2 cup pasta
- ½ cup diced celery
- 1 cup thawed frozen carrots and peas
- ½ tsp. dried leaf basil
- A dash of garlic powder
- 1 tsp. dried parsley flakes

Preparation Time: 8 hours
Yields: Serves 4 to 6

Instructions:

1. Add chicken, water, tomatoes, onions, celery, garlic powder, basil, parsley and chicken broth in the slow cooker. Let it cook for 5 to 7 hours on low.
2. Boil the pasta in salted water according to the instructions on the packet. A minute before the pasta is done, add the frozen vegetables. Drain and add it to the slow cooker and cook for an additional hour on low. Serve hot.

16. Split Pea Soup

Served with crusty bread or cornbread, this split pea soup is definitely a perfect choice for dinner when you want something simple, healthy and hearty.

Ingredients:

- 1 packet rinsed dried split peas (16 oz.)
- ½ cup chopped onions
- ¼ cup fresh chopped parsley
- 2 cups diced ham
- 3 sliced carrots
- 2 chopped celery ribs
- 1 bay leaf
- 2 minced garlic clove
- ½ tsp. fresh pepper
- 1 ½ quarts hot water
- 1 tbsp. salt

Preparation Time: 10 hours
Yields: Serves 8

Instructions:

1. Add all the ingredients to the slow cooker with the water and cook on low for 8 to 10 hours. Remove the bay leaf and mash the peas with spoon. Serve with croutons.

17. Turkey and Potato Soup

An excellent combination of turkey and some vegetables, this soup is rich and delicious in taste.

Ingredients:

- 4 cups chicken broth
- ½ cup chopped onions
- 5 medium diced potatoes
- 1 cup smoked turkey breast, chopped into cubes
- 1 cup shredded cheddar cheese
- 1 packet thawed and dried frozen spinach (10 oz.)
- ½ tsp. salt
- Pepper to taste
- 1 tsp. dry mustard

Preparation Time: 8 hours
Yields: Serves 6

Instructions:

1. In the slow cooker, add all the ingredients except the cheese and spinach. Cook for 7 to 8 hours on low. Add spinach and cook for another 20 minutes. Sprinkle with cheese and serve hot.

18. Winter Vegetable Beef Soup

In cold winter, this hearty soup recipe is ideal to give you some warmth and make you feel full.

Ingredients:

- 1 can stewed tomatoes (28 oz.)
- 1 lb. ground lean beef
- 1 can tomato sauce (15 oz.)
- 1 cup water
- 2 cups beef broth
- 1 envelope dry onion soup mix
- 2 cups frozen mixed vegetables

Preparation Time: 9 hours
Yields: Serves 4

Instructions:

1. Cook the meat in a large skillet until brown. Add it to the slow cooker along with other ingredients and cook for 7 to 9 hours on low.

19. Quick Beer Cheese Soup

If you want to add a little zing to your soup, a dash of beer is just what you need to make the perfect recipe.

Ingredients:

- 1 cup beer
- 2 cans cream of celery soup
- 16 oz. shredded cheddar cheese
- ¼ tsp. paprika
- 1 tsp. Worcestershire sauce

Preparation Time: 2 hours
Yields: Serves 2

Instructions:

1. Add all the ingredients to a slow cooker and cook for two hours on high. Stir occasionally. Serve with croutons.

20. Pasta Fagiole Soup

This is another Italian-tasting soup in this recipe book that is definitely going to make your mouth water.

Ingredients:

- 1 cup chopped onions
- 2 cans chicken broth
- 1 can drained and rinsed white kidney beans
- 2/3 cup cooked macaroni
- 5 chopped garlic cloves
- 1 can tomatoes (28 oz.)
- 1 tbsp. olive oil
- Grated cheese to taste
- Salt and pepper to taste
- Chopped parsley to taste

Preparation Time: 4 hours
Yields: Serves 6 to 8

Instructions:

1. In a skillet, saute the garlic and onion in oil for about a minute. Add this to the slow cooker along with chopped tomatoes, broth, salt, pepper and parsley. Cook on low for 3 hours.
2. Add beans and cooked macaroni to the cooker, adjust the seasonings and cook on low for another 30 minutes. Serve with grated cheese.

21. Tortilla Soup

Another great tasting soup recipe that you definitely need to try is the slow cooker tortilla soup that is light and unique in taste.

Ingredients:

- 1 finely chopped onion
- 2 skinned halves of chicken breast, diced into cubes
- 4 cups chicken broth
- 3 medium peeled and chopped tomatoes
- 1 crushed garlic clove
- 4 corn tortillas cut into ¼ inch strips
- 1 chopped green chili
- Salt and pepper to taste
- 2 tbsp. vegetable oil
- 2 tbsp. chopped parsley
- Shredded Monterey Cheese for serving

Preparation Time: 8 hours
Yields: Serves 4

Instructions:

1. In a slow cooker, add chicken, broth, tomatoes, garlic, onion, green chili, salt and pepper. Cook for 7 to 8 hours on low.
2. In another pan heat oil and add tortilla strips to it. Cook on medium heat until they turn crisp and then drain on paper towels.
3. Ladle the soup into bowls, and add tortilla strips and cheese on top.

22. Hamburger Soup

If you love eating hamburgers, why not try a healthier alternative? The delicious hamburger soup.

Ingredients:

- 1 lb. lean ground beef
- 1 cup cooked macaroni
- 1 cup sliced carrots
- 1 cup sliced celery
- 1 can tomato sauce (8 oz.)
- 1 beef bouillon cube
- 3 cups boiling water
- ¼ cup grated cheese
- 1 envelope dry onion soup mix
- 1 tbsp. soy sauce
- ¼ tsp. salt
- ¼ tsp. oregano
- ¼. tsp. basil
- ¼ tsp. pepper

Preparation Time: 8 hours
Yields: Serves 6

Instructions:

1. Add all the ingredients except macaroni and cheese in a slow cooker. Cook for 6 to 8 hours on low.
2. Add cheese and macaroni to the slow cooker and cook for another 15 minutes on high. Serve hot.

23. Ground Turkey Soup

Mixed with some vegetables and served with some Italian seasonings, this turkey soup recipe is amazing in taste!

Ingredients:

- 1 lb. ground turkey
- 1 cup chopped onions
- 1 cup diced carrots
- 1 cup diced celery
- 1 cup diced green pepper
- 1 cup tomato sauce
- 3 cups boiling water
- 1 cup sliced mushrooms
- 1 tbsp. soy sauce
- 3 tsp. beef bouillon
- ¼ tsp. oregano
- ¼ tsp. pepper
- ¼ tsp. basil
- 2 tbsp. butter

Preparation Time: 8 hours
Yields: Serves 4 to 6

Instructions:

1. Saute mushrooms and turkey in butter in a pan until the turkey is browned. Add it to the slow cooker with all other ingredients and cook for 6 to 8 hours on low. Serve with garlic bread.

24. Asparagus Soup

Asparagus is definitely a healthy thing to eat so why not make delicious soup out of it? Try this and you'll definitely be hooked.

Ingredients:

- 5 cups chicken broth
- 2 cups peeled and cubed baking potatoes
- 6 finely chopped green onions
- 2 lbs. fresh asparagus
- ¼ tsp. ground pepper
- ¼ tsp. salt

Preparation Time: 8 hours
Yields: Serves 4

Instructions:

1. Cut off the woody ends of the asparagus and rinse the spears. Chop the asparagus into 1-inch pieces.
2. In a slow cooker, add asparagus, green onions, broth and potatoes. Cook for 5 to 7 hours on low.
3. Take out the vegetables and turn the cooker on high. In a blender, puree the vegetables and add them back to the cooker. Add salt and pepper, and cook on high for another 30 minutes. Serve with parsley.

25. Chili Soup with Pinto Beans and Ground Beef

Served with a simple tossed salad and freshly baked cornbread, this delicious soup makes for a very hearty and satisfying dinner.

Ingredients:

- 1 lb. ground beef
- 1 can drained and rinsed pinto beans (15 oz.)
- 1 can tomatoes (28 oz.)
- 1 large chopped onion
- 1 can chopped chili pepper (4 oz.)
- 3 tbsp. chili powder
- 1 tsp. pepper
- Salt to taste

Preparation Time: 8 hours
Yields: Serves 4 to 6

Instructions:

1. Add all the ingredients in a slow cooker and cook for 6 to 8 hours on low. Adjust the seasoning and serve hot.

Conclusion

Now that you have these 25 delicious slow cooker recipes, there is no reason for you to wait for the weekend to cook delicious homemade hearty food that you and your family can enjoy. From beans to beef, you can enjoy every flavor at its best with these recipes. All you have to do is leave them cooking when you go for work and they'll be all nice and ready when you get back.

These simple recipes will make you an expert on slow cooker soups, letting you enjoy yummy soup at home whenever you feel like having it.

Your feedback is important to us. It would be greatly appreciated if you could please take a moment to REVIEW this book on Amazon so that we could make our next version better

CPSIA information can be obtained
at www.ICGtesting.com
Printed in the USA
BVOW06s2153181216

471198BV00001B/47/P